Here to Help

REFUSE COLLECTOR

Rachel Blount

Photography by Bobby Humphrey

W

FRANKLIN WATTS

LONDON • SYDNEY

Franklin Watts
First published in Great Britain in 2016 by The Watts Publishing Group

Credits
Series Editors: Rachel Blount and Paul Humphrey
Series Designer: D. R. ink
Photographer: Bobby Humphrey
Produced for Franklin Watts by Discovery Books Ltd.
Photo credits: Shutterstock: p18 middle, urbanbuzz.

Every attempt has been made to clear copyright. Should there be any inadvertent omission
please apply to the publisher for rectification.

Dewey number: 628.442
HB ISBN: 978 1 4451 4030 8
Library eBook ISBN: 978 1 4451 4031 5

Printed in China

Franklin Watts
An imprint of
Hachette Children's Group
Part of The Watts Publishing Group
Carmelite House
50 Victoria Embankment
London EC4Y 0DZ

An Hachette UK Company
www.hachette.co.uk

www.franklinwatts.co.uk

The publisher and packager would like to thank Terence Richardson, Jess Ward, Mike Stass,
Paul Farmer and staff at FCC Environment; Wychavon District Council; Severn Waste Services.

Contents

Words in **bold** are in the glossary on page 24.

I am a refuse collector

Hello!

I'm Jess.

My name is Tex and I am a refuse collector. It is my job to drive the refuse truck, collect rubbish and **recycling** from people's houses and take it to the recycling centre or **landfill site**.

I work with Jess. She is a **loader**. It is her job to attach the rubbish bins to the back of the refuse truck.

This is Adrian. He is my **supervisor**.
He works in the office at the **depot**.

Sam is one of the **managers**. He helps to organise all of the refuse collectors in the area.

?

Have you seen refuse collectors working where you live? What colour was the refuse truck?

My uniform

At work I wear a **uniform**. I wear safety boots and trousers, a T-shirt and a **high-visibility** vest. The safety trousers protect my legs if there is any broken glass or sharp objects in the rubbish.

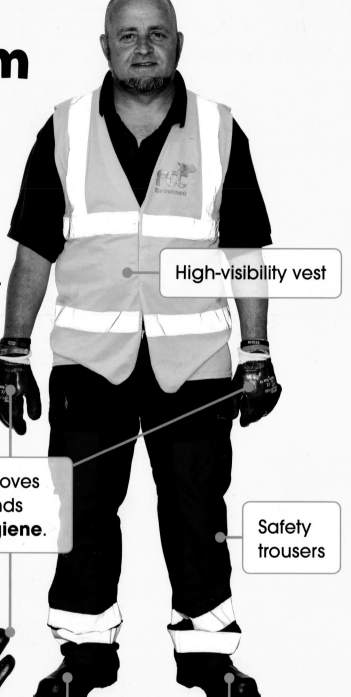

High-visibility vest

Gloves – I wear gloves to protect my hands and for good **hygiene**.

Safety trousers

Safety boots

I also wear a hard hat when I am outside the truck at the recycling centre or landfill site.

These are the wheelie bins we collect in this area. Green bins are for waste that can be recycled, such as paper, plastic and glass. Black bins are for household waste that cannot be recycled and goes into landfill sites. Brown bins are for garden waste.

Recycling

Household waste

Garden waste

What colour refuse bins, bags or boxes do you have where you live?

The refuse truck

This is the refuse truck that I drive.

Warning lights

Cab

Mirrors

There are large mirrors on the sides of the cab so that I can see where Jess is working.

?

Why is it important for the driver to see the loader working at the back of the truck?

The warning lights on the top and the back of the truck flash when the truck is working. The truck beeps loudly when it is **reversing**, too.

Safety barriers

Bin lift

Emergency stop button

Manual controls

Inside the cab there are buttons to work the back of the truck. There is a camera monitor, too. This helps the driver to see the loaders when they are at the back of the truck.

Camera monitor

Safety first

It is 6:00 am and time to go. I grab the keys and head to the refuse truck with Jess.

I check the lights and windscreen wipers are working properly, then I check the mirrors and the oil.

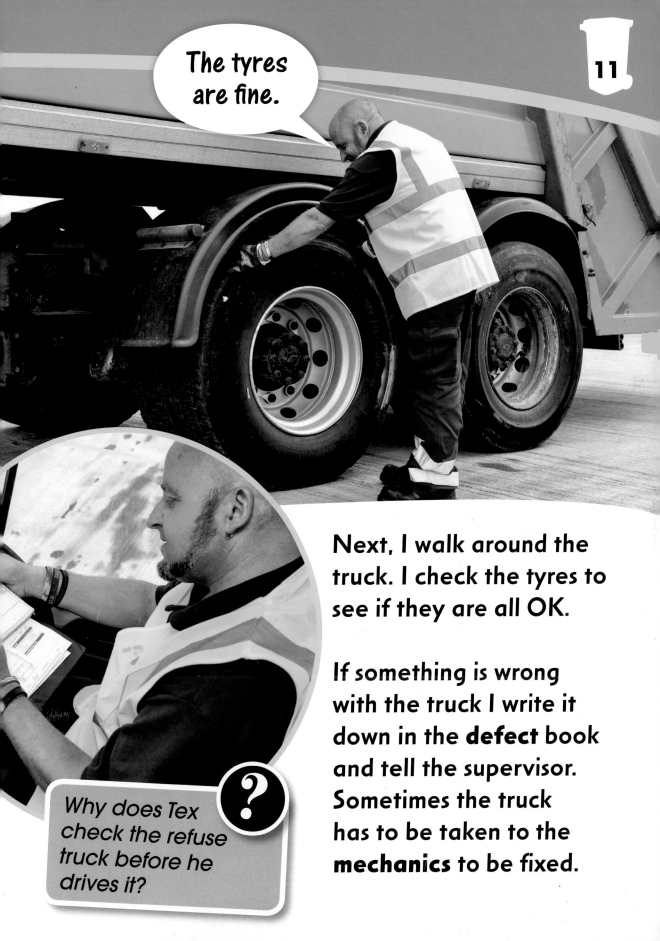

The tyres are fine.

Why does Tex check the refuse truck before he drives it?

Next, I walk around the truck. I check the tyres to see if they are all OK.

If something is wrong with the truck I write it down in the **defect** book and tell the supervisor. Sometimes the truck has to be taken to the **mechanics** to be fixed.

Time to go

We are collecting the recycling today. Jess gets out of the cab and directs me into the first road. It is quite hard to see where I am going when I am reversing the truck.

This way Tex.

I park the truck and get out to help Jess wheel the bins to the back of the truck.

?

How many bins do you think Tex and Jess collect in one day?

When the bin is in place the truck lifts it up, tips it out and brings it back down **automatically**. This happens quite quickly. We stand behind the safety barriers so that we won't get hurt if a bin slips off.

Metal plate

Inside the truck a big metal plate scoops the recycling up and squashes it to make space for more to be collected.

Contaminated recycling

Next, we empty some large recycling bins from a block of flats. Everyone who lives here puts their rubbish into big, **communal** bins.

One of the recycling bins has flies around it. I take a look inside and see it has landfill waste mixed in with the recycling waste.

There are nappies in this recycling bin.

We cannot empty this bin today because it will **contaminate** the rest of the recycling we have collected. It will be emptied next week and go into landfill.

Back in the cab Jess completes a **report** about the contaminated bin. This is a record for the managers and office staff in case anyone rings up and complains.

?

Why does Jess fill in a report in the cab?

Dropping off the recycling

When the truck is full I drive to the recycling centre. The truck is weighed when I arrive and when I leave to see how much recycling we have collected.

Hello Tex.

I reverse the truck into the bay to empty the load.

I press a button to open the back of the truck. The metal plate pushes the recycling out. A digger will push the rubbish into huge piles before it is lifted onto a **conveyor belt** and sorted.

When we are collecting household waste I empty the truck at the landfill site. It is quite smelly here!

? Why does it smell at the landfill site?

There are bulldozers at the site that flatten the rubbish.

Other jobs

These are some of the other vehicles I drive at work. This small refuse truck can fit down narrow lanes.

Some people dump their rubbish in places where it is not allowed. This is called **fly-tipping**. I use a big truck like this one when we have to clear up large pieces of rubbish.

This is a road sweeper truck. It has a brush that sweeps along the edges of roads to clean up any rubbish and dirt. Smaller road sweepers are used to clean pavements and high streets.

Have you seen a sweeper truck working? If so, what noise did it make?

Brush

The end of the day

Once the truck is empty I drive back to the depot. It has been a busy day but I still have some jobs to do.

I take the truck to the wash bay. Every day the truck has to be washed and cleaned, ready for the next day.

Next, I refuel the truck. Then I write down the time and weight of the vehicle on my **time sheets**.

Why does Tex write down the time on his time sheets?

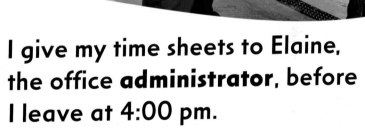

I give my time sheets to Elaine, the office **administrator**, before I leave at 4:00 pm.

Here are my time sheets, Elaine.

Helping people

I really enjoy my job working outdoors as a refuse collector. I've found some strange things in the rubbish! Most of all I enjoy helping to keep the streets where we live clean and tidy.

When you grow up...

If you would like to be a refuse collector, here are some simple tips and advice.

What kind of person are you?

- You enjoy working as part of a team
- You are friendly and enjoy talking to the public
- You don't mind getting dirty
- Most of all, you enjoy helping people.

How do you become a refuse collector?

You don't need any special qualifications to become a refuse collector. You can look and apply for jobs through council websites or waste management companies.

You need to pass a heavy goods vehicle driving test to be able to drive a refuse truck.

You can complete a specialist waste and environment management course at some universities.

You could study business management, accounting or sales and work in these areas of waste and recycling.

Answers

P8. The driver needs to see the loader on the camera monitor in the cab and in the mirrors to check that they are safe.

P11. Tex checks the truck to make sure it is safe to drive.

P12. On a normal day Tex and Jess collect between 1,000 and 2,000 bins!

P15. Jess fills in a report in the cab so that the incident is recorded straight away and sent to the office staff at the depot.

P17. Landfill sites contain household waste, such as dirty nappies, rotting food and dog waste, amongst other things that are very smelly.

P21. Tex records the time because he has stopped driving the truck. Drivers of heavy goods trucks are only allowed to drive for a set number of hours in a day. This means they are safe and not tired.

Were your answers the same as the ones in this book? Don't worry if they were different, sometimes there is more than one right answer. Talk about your answer with other people. Can you explain why you think your answer is right?

Glossary

administrator someone who is responsible for carrying out the administration of a business

automatically without being instructed

cab the front part of the refuse truck where the driver and loader sit

communal shared with other people in the area

contaminate to make dirty or pollute

conveyor belt a continuous moving belt that transports objects from one place to another

defect fault

depot a place where the refuse trucks are kept when they are not being used and where people work in the office

fly-tipping dumping rubbish where it is not allowed. Fly-tipping is illegal and people can be fined if they are caught

high-visibility easy to see

hygiene preventing disease through cleanliness

landfill site a hole in the ground where rubbish is collected and then buried

loader someone who works on the refuse truck. Their job is to attach the wheelie bins and empty them into the truck

managers people who are in charge of an organisation or group of people

mechanics people who repair and maintain vehicles

recycling the process of changing certain waste materials so that they can be used again

report a written account

reversing going backwards

supervisor someone who is in charge of a small group of people

time sheets a record of the amount of time a driver has driven a vehicle

uniform special clothing worn by people who belong to the same organisation

Index